The PROFIT MINDSET

Know Your Numbers, Plan Ahead, Grow Your Business

ANDY CRISTIN

R^ethink

First published in Great Britain in 2020
by Rethink Press (www.rethinkpress.com)

Cover image © Shutterstock | graficriver_icons_logo/ Lidiia Koval

Contents

Introduction

Successful entrepreneurs create businesses which they can grow profitably and eventually sell. Some then repeat the exercise, becoming serial entrepreneurs. But for every successful serial entrepreneur there are many, many business owners whose businesses have plateaued. After the initial euphoria of setting up their own business, and all the hard work that is required to achieve an initial level of success, most of these business owners cannot continue to scale their businesses.

You might not be looking to be the next Richard Branson, but running your own business is risky and hard work. You should at least be able to get a better return for your time and effort than you would do in an equivalent job; however, the numbers are against you. Most people have heard the statistic that 60% of businesses fail within the first five years. But that is just the tip of the iceberg. Only 25% of businesses ever grow to the point where they can hire their first staff member.[1] Just 4% will achieve a revenue of £1 million or more.[2] More than 40% of transactions in the average business do not

1   Department for Business, Energy & Industrial Strategy (2019) 'Business population estimates for the UK and regions: 2019 statistical release', www.gov.uk/government/publications/business-population-estimates-2019/business-population-estimates-for-the-uk-and-regions-2019-statistical-release-html, accessed 5 January 2020

2   P Wetherill, et al (2018) 'UK business; activity, size and location: 2018', Office for National Statistics, www.ons.gov.uk/businessindustryandtrade/business/activitysizeandlocation/bulletins/ukbusinessactivitysizeandlocation/2018, accessed 7 August 2020

make a profit[3] and less than 20% of businesses listed for sale will ever find a buyer.[4]

Clearly, the average business owner has the odds stacked against them. Their goals might be to make money, own a business that runs itself and eventually sell it for a significant amount of money. Unfortunately, it is more likely that they will work long hours, feel stressed out and earn less than their salaried peers.

A number of classic business books, such as *The E-Myth Revisited*[5] and *The Beermat Entrepreneur*,[6] describe a successful company structure as

---

3   JLS Byrnes (2010) *Islands of Profit in a Sea of Red Ink: Why 40% of your business is unprofitable, and how to fix it.* New York: Portfolio Penguin

4   R Parker (n.d.) 'Are you tired of trying to sell your business and it still not sold', thebusinessexchange .com, www.thebusinessexchange.co/the-seller-finance -specialists, accessed 31 August 2020

5   ME Gerber (2017) *The E-Myth Revisited: Why most small businesses don't work and what to do about it.* New York: Harperbusiness

6   M Southon and C West (2018) *The Beermat Entrepreneur: Turn your good idea into a great business.* London: Pearson Education

having three distinct disciplines. These disciplines are sales, service delivery and finance. Most entrepreneurs excel at sales or service delivery, but few go into business because they are good at accounting. This vital third of the business is often under-resourced and under-appreciated, which leads to poor growth and low profits.

Over the last twenty years I have worked alongside several entrepreneurs and serial entrepreneurs, providing financial advice to help them grow their businesses. I have also been a business owner going through the process of starting a business, growing sales and then selling the business in a trade sale. In all of these businesses, the finance function played a significant role in their success.

As a business owner you don't need to know how to run your finance function in detail, but your business will be much more successful if you understand a few key principles. This book gives you a method to develop a profit mindset. If you follow the four-step CASH method described in the following chapters, you will have confidence in your numbers, get laser-focused on profit, produce a simple and coherent three-year plan, and significantly increase your chances of executing that plan.

Running your business should be enjoyable and profitable. It should enable you to have greater confidence and control over your financial future while still having enough time to enjoy life outside work. Put the CASH method into action and improve the return on your business.

ONE

The SME Landscape

Starting a business is easier now than at any time in history. When I started my first limited company in 1995, it was still a requirement for most companies to have an annual audit by a firm of registered accountants. It cost hundreds of pounds just to get a company set up at Companies House, and everything was done on paper by a company-formation agency. Signed documents had to be passed back and forth by snail mail, taking days, if not weeks. You also needed to have a company secretary and a director. Today, anyone can set a company up online for about £25 and be ready to do business in a matter of hours.

In the year 2000 about 3.5 million businesses existed in the UK. By 2019 this number had grown to over 5.9 million.[7] However, while it is relatively easy to start a company it's not so easy to start and run a successful business. According to the Office for National Statistics, only about 60% of businesses will survive long enough to see their third birthday and only 40% survive for five years or longer.[8] The figures for businesses in the USA and Australia tell the same story.

---

7   Department for Business, Energy & Industrial Strategy, 'Business population estimates for the UK and regions: 2019 statistical release'

8   J Scruton (2017) 'Business demography, UK: 2017', Office for National Statistics, www.ons.gov.uk/businessindustryandtrade/business /activitysizeandlocation/bulletins/businessdemography /2017, accessed 7 August 2020

Perhaps more concerning is that only about 25% of businesses ever grow beyond one employee.[9] Therefore, three-quarters of all businesses are basically individuals who own a job. Most of these business owners would earn more money, be less stressed and have more free time if they went back to full-time employment.

If you have created a business which has lasted for three years or longer and you've managed to grow that business so that you employ a small team, you are already doing far better than the majority of your peers. But if you want to continue to grow your business and create an enterprise which is valuable, the odds are still very much against you.

According to a survey by the accounting software providers Xero, about two-thirds of the owners of failed businesses blame financial

---

9   Department for Business, Energy & Industrial Strategy, 'Business population estimates for the UK and regions: 2019 statistical release'

problems for their company's failure.[10] This is backed up by reports from the Australian Securities and Investment Commission, which publishes an analysis of business insolvencies in an annual review.[11] The most common causes of these insolvencies are inadequate cash flow, poor strategic management, poor financial control, and trading losses.

Even if you manage to build your business so that it has a significant turnover and a team of employees who do the day-to-day work, it is not necessarily going to be easy to sell that business – assuming that an exit is part of your plan. Only 10%–20% of businesses listed for

---

10   Xero (n.d.) 'Make or break? An investigation by Xero into what separates successful entrepreneurs from those who fail', Xero.com, www.xero.com/content/dam/xero/pdf /Xero-Make-or-break-report.pdf, accessed 2 August 2020, p. 7
11   Australian Securities and Investments Commission (2016) '16–436MR ASIC reports on corporate insolvencies 2015–16', https://asic.gov.au/about-asic/news-centre/find -a-media-release/2016-releases/16-436mr-asic-reports-on -corporate-insolvencies-2015-16, accessed 5 January 2020, Table 3

sale are believed to be successful in finding a buyer.[12]

There are some companies that beat the odds. I've been involved in eleven start-ups, all of which grew from nothing to become significant businesses. Four of them went on to have annual sales in excess of £1 million, and one went on to increase that figure to £100 million. All eleven of them saw their fifth birthday, and between them they employed over 1,000 people and were profitable. A key element of their success was that the founders of these businesses took the finance function seriously from the start.

In contrast, most owner-managed businesses rely on a bookkeeper to manage the day-to-day transactions and an external accountant to manage the compliance (producing the annual statutory accounts for Companies House and

---

12   R Parker, 'Are you tired of trying to sell your business and it still not sold'

completing the tax return for HM Revenue and Customs). That external accountant will usually visit the business no more than once a year. They will never get to know the business to the extent that they can provide management advice.

The more strategic finance work, such as analysing financial results and producing long-term financial plans, does not generally happen in smaller entities. Often the only profit reporting that these businesses see is a set of annual accounts, which are primarily prepared for the benefit of the tax authorities. Worse still, these accounts are usually not available until many months after the period to which they relate. Managing a business with this information is a bit like driving a car while focusing solely on the rear-view mirror.

This lack of internal financial understanding is a key reason that most businesses fail to break the £1 million barrier or go on to be truly profitable.

TWO

Profit Principles

The best entrepreneurs have a good overview of how their finance functions work without ever getting involved in the detail. Their understanding at a conceptual level provides them with a structure of mental models that help them make consistent, profit-based decisions. For example, if you have a clear view of your ideal client profile and you are also clear on what is core and non-core business, you will be focused on attracting the right kind of work. You won't waste time chasing unsuitable work, unlike a competitor who is operating without that clarity.

Here are some of the key concepts that successful businesses use, either deliberately or by chance.

Start with small data, not big data

If you're running Facebook, you need access to an enormous amount of data. The algorithms used to target their advertising are beyond the comprehension of most people. The quantity of data that they process for more than two billion subscribers is enormous. They have thousands of employees using vast amounts of computer power to measure, analyse and project who is likely to buy what and when.

If you are reading this book, you are more likely to be running a business with sales of less than £10 million a year. Getting an initial understanding of your key numbers is going to be far more useful to you. Every business is different, but these numbers might include generic key performance indicators (KPIs) such as revenue per employee, cost per unit, gross profit margin and debtor days.

Profit, not revenue

A common error is to concentrate too much on the top-line revenue number. While this problem will not be news to most people, it is surprising how much decision-making is influenced by this figure alone. This is at least partly because revenue is much easier to measure than the more important figure of profit.

Research by Jonathan Byrnes at the Massachusetts Institute of Technology suggests that most businesses are spending the majority of their time doing work that is not really profitable. In his book *Islands of Profit in a Sea of Red Ink*, Byrnes states that 40% of business transactions are unprofitable, while 20%–30% are so profitable that they subsidise the losses. The remainder are marginally profitable at best.[13]

Most companies would actually be more profitable if they shrank to a fraction of their current size. I have certainly seen examples of this. To confidently grow your business it is vital to understand where your profit comes from, but most businesses are unable to do·so. Who is responsible for profit in your business?

Focus on the big stuff

Most people are time poor, so you need to focus the time you do have on the areas where you can make the biggest difference. One tool that will help you with this is the 80/20 principle,

---

13   JLS Byrnes, *Islands of Profit in a Sea of Red Ink: Why 40% of your business is unprofitable, and how to fix it*

also known as the Pareto Principle.[14] It states that there is generally unequal distribution in the world. Outputs do not directly correlate to inputs. The ratio 80/20 refers to a rule of thumb that 80% of the outputs come from only 20% of the related inputs. For example, the top 20% of your customers provide you with 80% of your revenue. It could be 70/20 or 90/5, but the principle still holds.

While this rule is widely recognised, it is not well understood or applied. Most managing directors are guilty of spending too much time and effort on the wrong 80% at times.

---

14   K Kruse (n.d.) 'The 80/20 rule and how it can change your life', *Forbes*, www.forbes.com/sites/kevinkruse /2016/03/07/80-20-rule/#6a8f3b433814, accessed 31 August 2020

Rational thinking

Most people think that their decisions, especially business decisions, are based on rational thought. Frequently that is not the case.

In your own business, it's easy to get too close to the details and make decisions with your heart rather than your head. While this may sometimes be appropriate, too many projects start without a rational business case or continue long after a rational mind would have closed them down. An independent adviser is more likely to see the big picture and identify the errors in such decisions. It's less easy to do so when you're working in the business every day. If you don't have an external adviser or sounding board to question some of your decisions, it is easy to go off track.

Structure (automated systems)

While serving as president of the United States of America, Barack Obama only wore blue or grey suits and white shirts. His reasoning was that he didn't want to waste any mental energy on deciding what to wear every morning. It saved time and effort to restrict the options available, and he needed to conserve that mental capacity for more important matters. His administration was structured so that the majority of the decisions were made by someone else in his team and only the really big decisions would reach his desk.

This is how an efficient business should work. A successful leader will rarely have to get involved in day-to-day issues when they have a coherent plan that has been communicated clearly to competent staff; robust systems for sales, operations and finance; and a high level of automation.

THREE

The Three Big Mistakes

Before we look at the CASH method in detail, it's worth considering the problems that led to its creation. In the corporate world, I had always worked with businesses that had good data. When you have good data you can produce accurate reports and make informed decisions. With that data and reporting, it's relatively easy to plan ahead.

It was an eye-opener when I first started working with small- and medium-sized enterprises

(SMEs). Most of these organisations had only basic accounting functions. It was a common scenario to have a relatively unqualified book-keeper managing all the day-to-day accounting. This bookkeeper would then report directly to the business owner, who was also unqualified and inexperienced in finance. Regular, accurate reporting was rare in these companies.

The three things that were clearly missing from these organisations were:

1. A good understanding of the numbers

2. A laser focus on profit

3. Planning for the future

As I drill down into these three frequently over-looked aspects of financial management, I have twelve questions to enable you to assess your current capability in these areas.

A good understanding of the numbers

Most SMEs do not have sufficient financial systems and expertise to give them a clear understanding of their business numbers. For example, a set of monthly management accounts, which is normal in a large business, was rarely available in the SMEs I started working with. Decisions were generally based on gut feelings rather than a rational analysis of good-quality data. That's like trying to drive a car at the speed limit without being able to see the speedometer.

An example of this issue is a company I worked with in the construction industry. The managers were unable to measure the revenue that the company earned in a particular period. They were involved in long-term building projects and were only able to invoice their clients after certain milestones were achieved. It was not unusual to have a twelve-month project with one invoice raised every three months.

Consequently, the sales figure in their management accounts did not reflect the revenue they had earned in the month. As a result, their reported profits see-sawed up and down and the management had no chance of understanding the company's true performance so that they could make informed decisions.

HOW WELL DOES YOUR BUSINESS UNDERSTAND THE NUMBERS?

Answer the four questions below, scoring 1 for yes and 0 for no.

1. Do you know your net profit margin as a percentage?

2. Do you know your break-even point?

3. Do you produce regular management accounts?

4. Do you understand the cash flow in your business?

It's virtually impossible for a business to make sound, profitable decisions unless there are systems to produce good data – both financial and non-financial. Putting these systems in place is like getting the foundations right before you build the house.

A laser focus on profit

As businesses grow, they become more complex. Initially, there may only be one product, one price, one sales channel and one delivery method. However, as time goes on and revenue increases, the business becomes more complicated. In most SMEs, the systems simply don't exist to analyse the profitability across all the different activities. Expansion then leads the business to take on increasingly diverse work with a diminishing understanding of what makes a profit.

I came across this problem early in my career, working for a large logistics business. Their clients ranged from small family-run retail units to large national chains. Most of the directors believed that the national chains provided good profits despite the price discounts they were given due to the volume of their business. However, when the finance director asked me to analyse the profitability of the largest clients, it was clear that this was not the case. Most of the large national chains were only marginally profitable and one household name was actually making a significant loss. This had gone on for many years but until the analysis was done the losses were invisible, even in a relatively sophisticated business.

HOW FOCUSED ON PROFITABILITY IS YOUR BUSINESS?

Answer the four questions below, scoring 1 for yes and 0 for no.

1. Do you know your gross margin as a percentage?

2. Do you analyse your gross margin by product (or service)?

3. Do you know how profitable your top five clients are?

4. Is your business more profitable than most of its competitors?

When any business starts to get complex there are likely to be elements that are not profitable. Unless these are identified and either corrected or removed, the business will plateau, doing lots of work for a poor return.

Planning for the future

When SMEs do not have clarity in their numbers, planning becomes more difficult. Most small businesses do not even produce a forecast profit and loss account for the next twelve months. Without a coherent plan, the business has no benchmark to measure progress against. Management cannot be held responsible for delivering on promises, and nasty cash flow surprises are more likely to creep up on the business.

A large services contractor that I work with is a good example of the benefits of such planning. They had not previously done any long-term planning so, using one of the tools outlined in this book, we produced a forecast for the next three years. The owner wasn't looking for huge growth every year (around 10%), but they wanted to be more profitable. By mapping out the three years, it became clear that the organisational structure needed to change and the size of the average contract needed to double, otherwise the contract management costs would hold back profitability growth. Three years later the organisational structure had been put in place, the average contract size had more than doubled and the company was enjoying much better profitability.

HOW GOOD IS YOUR BUSINESS PLANNING?

Answer the four questions below, scoring 1 for yes and 0 for no.

1. Do you produce annual budgets?

2. Do you have a cash flow forecast?

3. Do you have a three-year plan?

4. Do you have a marketing plan to support your growth ambitions?

A business plan does not have to be long and complicated. A simple plan will be worth its weight in gold if it helps you see where you are going. Most people would not go on their annual holiday or get married without a plan, so why would you try to run a business without one?

How did you score for the twelve questions above? If your score was less than eight out of twelve, you need to read on.

FOUR

Introduction To The CASH Method

This book is based on a four-step method that I have developed over many years. After spending the early part of my career working in large international companies, I began working for smaller, owner-managed businesses and found it much more interesting. Being able to make decisions in the morning and implement them in the afternoon was refreshing after working for larger, more bureaucratic enterprises. However, the decision-making processes were generally much weaker.

Most of these owner-managed firms had annual sales of less than £10 million and employed less than 100 people. None of them could afford, or needed, a full-time finance director, but they could all benefit from having access to one for a few days a month. They came from a variety of sectors, but their financial problems were often similar. Some key themes were:

- Managing cash flow
- Improving profitability
- Growing the business
- Planning an exit

Most of them also had no one to act as a sounding board. Life as the owner of a small business is a lonely place to be, and having someone to bounce ideas off makes a positive difference.

I have been lucky enough to work with some great clients over the years. From those experiences, I formulated the four-step method to enable SME owners to know their numbers, plan ahead and grow their businesses. This method has a memorable acronym: CASH. The four steps are:

1. Clarify your numbers

2. Analyse the profit

3. Set growth objectives

4. Hit your targets

Step One: Clarify your numbers

Some businesses need to start with the basics of identifying and capturing the correct raw data. Others already have sophisticated accounting systems but need help designing reports and identifying KPIs to manage the business. This step involves a lot of technical accounting work to ensure that the information coming out of the accounting system is a good foundation for reporting and for making decisions.

As a business owner, this is not a good use of your time. However, once you have a system producing good-quality financial information, it is important that you understand the key numbers. Aim for six KPIs which monitor the main areas of your business.

Step Two: Analyse the profit

Here we look at two key elements of your business model: your core business and your ideal client profile.

Many businesses lose their focus after a few years and stray into non-core work that returns a relatively low profit. This non-core work is also likely to generate a high level of problems for the business. Another error is working for clients who do not fit the ideal client profile. SMEs need to focus on strictly defined client types rather than chasing business from anyone and everyone.

The object in this step is to identify the services and clients that provide above-average profits. It sounds simple, but according to the research most businesses make little or no profit on the majority of their sales transactions.[15]

Step Three: Set growth objectives

Once you have good-quality information on your business performance and you have identified the profit-generating activities, the next step is to produce a three-year plan to take the business forward.

The central assumption here will be the sales revenue projected over the next three years. At the same time, we need to ensure that the business has sufficient resources – such as staff,

---

15   JLS Byrnes, *Islands of Profit in a Sea of Red Ink: Why 40% of your business is unprofitable, and how to fix it*

offices, marketing and cash – to support that growth. The projected level of revenue growth should be both a stretch and achievable, while making sure that you attain an acceptable profit.

Step Four: Hit your targets

It's great to have a plan, but the exercise is pointless unless that plan is well executed. In the final step, we will look at some tools and procedures to help you stay on track and ensure that you are regularly held to account for executing your plan.

To illustrate how the CASH method worked in a fast-growing business, I have included a case study of my first start-up. This case study looks at the four steps of the CASH method, so it is included in parts at the end of the next four chapters.

CASE STUDY PART ONE: '44 MILLION TEA BAGS, 30 MILLION EGGS AND 3 MILLION LOAVES OF BREAD'

While I was working in one of my first roles as an accountant my company received a tender to manage a logistics contract serving 1,700 catering outlets in various parts of the world. This would be a huge contract for us, much bigger than any other client. The company, along with some of our competitors, decided to respond to this tender, despite the general thinking that the incumbent would retain the business and that the tender process was merely a price-checking exercise.

We set up a small team to produce the tender response, all of us seconded from our usual roles. Graeme was the team leader. He was an experienced sales manager who previously looked after large national accounts, including high street chains. Neil was responsible for the operations. His role was to map out the logistical requirements and design an infrastructure to deliver the services. I was in charge of finance: producing a forecast of costs, revenue and cash flows. We were set the task of producing a credible response to the tender which would also provide the company with a profit.

While there were other elements to the business, the three of us covered the core functions of a business as described in *The E-Myth*: sales, service delivery and finance.

After submitting our bid document, we were the only other candidate to make it through to the final round, along with the incumbent. Three weeks later, we were awarded the contract. I can still clearly remember the phone call from Graeme to say 'We've got it!'

The award caused a fair amount of publicity at the time, with the news being reported by the *Financial Times*.

At that point, we had just six months to set the business up. In that time we needed to obtain two warehouses in the UK and one in mainland Europe, fit them out and take on more than 300 staff.

FIVE

C: Clarify Your Numbers

The first step in the CASH method is to clarify the numbers.

This step can involve a deep dive into some technical accounting areas, which takes time and is outside the scope of this book. Here we will concentrate on identifying the key numbers and ratios that you need to understand and monitor in order to grow a profitable business.

Understanding the numbers is critical to managing any business. Every successful owner I have worked with was familiar with the key numbers in their business. Even those who had hated maths at school knew exactly how their business numbers worked in the real world. Basic data, such as sales, payroll costs and cash in the bank, is a good start, but a better understanding comes from measuring ratios and percentages and finding relationships between the numbers.

A good example from the hotel industry is the occupancy rate, which is expressed as a percentage. If a hotel has one hundred rooms and eighty-five of them are occupied on a particular night, the occupancy rate is 85%. This figure can be compared to the rate in other hotels, or the same period in the previous year, and it will give some explanation of the trading results. A hotel expert could probably look at the occupancy rate alone and have a good idea of whether the hotel is profitable or not, even though this KPI is non-financial.

Some key metrics are rather niche. I once did some consultancy for a large automotive repair business that refurbished hire cars at the end of the rental period. It was a fiercely competitive market, and profit margins were low. The work involved checking and repairing cars before they were sent to auction. In the costings reports produced by their accountant there was an income line called 'small change'. When I asked what this was, I was told that when cleaning each vehicle, on average they would find £2.30 in loose change which had been lost down the back of the seats. That might sound like a small or arbitrary amount, but when the price of a basic service was less than £100 and profit margins were low, it was actually an important figure to measure and understand.

Research from the Association of Accounting Technicians shows that SMEs are particularly poor at resourcing finance staff. They estimate that nearly £3 billion a year is lost by UK SMEs because 'finance is not being taken seriously enough by aspiring business owners'.[16]

---

16 Association of Accounting Technicians (2015) 'Small and medium businesses "leaking" £2.9 billion due to unqualified finance staff', www.aat.org.uk/news/article

If you don't take the time to understand your business numbers, you are likely to:

1. Suffer lower profitability
2. Waste time being inefficient
3. Endure higher stress levels

To understand why you need to know your numbers, just watch an episode of the BBC series *Dragons' Den*. In this programme, entrepreneurs get the chance to pitch their business ideas to five experienced investors in the hope that they will be able to raise funds to expand their business. You won't have to watch for long before you see a cringeworthy moment when an entrepreneur is asked a simple question about their numbers. On hearing 'What is your gross margin/net profit/cost per unit?', previously confident presenters can go completely blank or, worse still, talk through a list of numbers which are clearly inconsistent with each other and with earlier parts of their presentation. On the

---

/small-and-medium-businesses-leaking-29-billion-due -unqualified-finance-staff, accessed 2 August 2020

rare occasion when an entrepreneur presents an investable business and can answer questions on their numbers, they stand out like a genius.

Given that the programme first aired in the UK in 2005, anyone appearing on the show now must surely have watched a few episodes and realised the importance of getting the numbers right. Being able to present their figures with confidence is a key element to impressing the Dragons and getting the funds they require, but the same mistake is made time and again. Relatively basic questions about key numbers still produce blank faces. In one episode, a pair of experienced entrepreneurs were completely floored by the question 'What is your gross margin?' They amended their first answer of 40% several times, reaching a high of 50% and a low of 10%, before the editor cut to the chase. Despite this, the pair were still made offers by all five investors.

Perhaps the Dragons didn't really expect or want the entrepreneurs to understand their numbers. By bringing financial skills to the party, along with their cash and contacts, the Dragons were able to obtain a larger slice of the business for themselves.

How well do you know your numbers?

A simple way to get to know your numbers is to write down the cost structure for every £100 of sales. Take a piece of paper, write down 'Sales' on the left-hand side and '£100' on the right-hand side. Under 'Sales', list five to ten major cost headings (eg staff, premises, equipment, sub-contractors, materials and professional fees). Then add 'Other costs' and finally 'Net profit'. Allocate the £100 against these headings without referring back to any reports. Finally, check the proportions you have written down against the figures your accountant produced in the most recent accounts. How accurate were you?

For a traditional taxi firm, the figures might look like this:

Sales	£100
Driver payroll	£61
Petrol	£11
Vehicle leases	£6
Admin payroll	£5
Premises costs (rent, rates, etc)	£4
Insurance	£2
Other costs	£4
Net profit	£7

In this case, the net profit for every £100 of sales is £7.

In the era of big data, large organisations measure just about everything and produce statistics for every part of their operation. They do this to ensure that each part of the business is monitored to improve performance. There are many examples of this in professional sports. Football produces dozens of statistics for every game played. If you watch an English Premier League game, you will probably be informed about:

- The number of shots
- The number of shots on target
- The ratio of shots to goals
- The number of passes
- The pass completion rate

I could easily list twenty more. Football teams use these numbers to identify strengths and weaknesses and even to value their players. These numbers are tools that focus attention on key areas of the game. Your business probably doesn't need dozens of statistics, but half a dozen key numbers will help you to focus on the most important areas.

What are the key metrics in your business?

Analysing the major costs in the example of the taxi business above is an important exercise, but more work is needed to get clarity. It is important to understand the relationships between your major cost groups, your business activities and the revenue that they generate. Include non-financial data to get a better picture.

For the fictional taxi business, the financial KPIs might include:

- Average fare value
- Vehicle running cost per mile
- Driver cost per hour

The non-financial KPIs might include:

- Number of fares per hour
- Average miles per hour
- The ratio of drivers to cars
- Vehicle down time

49

CASE STUDY PART TWO: CLARIFY THE NUMBERS

On this project, it was more a case of estimating the numbers than clarifying the numbers. This start-up was different from the classic entrepreneurial bootstrapping of a business from nothing. On the one hand, we were fortunate to have ready-made KPIs, systems and procedures for accounting. On the other hand, we had agreed the basis for our prices with the client in advance. The prices were 'fixed' for five years so that any increases had to follow a pre-set formula (eg for increases in diesel costs). We had to agree these before shipping the first order.

From a distance, logistics is a fairly simple business. Products are bought in bulk from manufacturers and arrive at one end of a warehouse. The goods are stacked in various sections of the warehouse.

Telesales operators phone each customer two or three times a week to take orders. Those orders are picked and moved to the loading area. The picked orders are then loaded onto trucks in the reverse order to which they are delivered (last in, first out). Finally, the drivers take each order to the customers.

For these activities, the operating KPIs we measured included:

- Orders taken per telesales operator

- Orders picked per warehouse operator

- Orders delivered per driver

Less obvious but equally important were:

- Miles driven per driver day

- Average order size

- Stock days

We knew that understanding our numbers would be vital to convince all our stakeholders that we could deliver on our proposal. We spent a lot of time checking and re-checking our assumptions and comparing our models with data from the existing business.

With various SMEs, I have completed similar processes to help them obtain bank finance, overdrafts and crowdfunded loans. I have also been involved in the due diligence process for business sales, where it is vital to show the purchaser that the company understands its numbers and monitors them carefully. Potential funders and purchasers will take a risk on your business only if they are convinced that the underlying numbers make sense. Why would you as an owner risk your time, effort, capital and future on a business unless you understand the numbers at the same level of detail?

SIX

A: Analyse The Profit

Once you are clear on your key business numbers, the second step in the CASH method is to answer the question: 'Where does my profit come from?' If your business only has one product or service and always sells this at the same price, this will be an easy exercise. However, businesses tend to get more complicated as they grow, adding further services, sales channels or discounts. It can become difficult to see which types of transaction are making a profit and which are making losses.

The full process involves a detailed analysis of the current business model, breaking down revenues and costs by client type, product or service, sales channel and geography. Here we will concentrate on two important elements of that analysis: core business and ideal clients.

While businesses often start with a limited number of services, as time goes on they can lose their focus on that core business. You might have a good client who asks you to provide a service you don't normally offer, because another supplier has let them down. This might seem like a good opportunity to expand, and you can then offer the additional non-core service to other clients. Another area where focus can slip is the type of clients that your business serves. Where once the profile of your ideal client was clear, you might lose this focus in a quest to expand the business based on revenue alone.

Before setting objectives for the future, it is important to define and communicate the business's niche in terms of its core services and ideal clients. Only once these two are clear in your mind should you plan to grow the business.

A good example of focus is a firm of insurance brokers who realised they were making these mistakes. They identified that clients who spent less than £2,000 a year with them were not aligned to their target client strategy. The firm provided a premium, personalised service and did not want to compete with other brokers who were providing web-enabled services. Over time, the firm encouraged the clients who did not fit their ideal profile to find a broker more able to respond to their needs and demands. The result was that the smaller, more focused business was much more profitable and efficient to run. A few years later they increased the acceptance threshold to £5,000 a year and continued to thrive.

Jonathan Byrnes' finding that 40% of trans-actions are unprofitable and 20%–30% are so profitable that they subsidise all the losses holds true when sales are analysed by client, service, geography and sales channel.[17] The problem SMEs have is that as their businesses grow and become more complex, they rarely have the data and reports to identify profitable and unprofitable activities.

This problem is common in the one-stop-shop business model. In the twentieth century, department stores were popular. Buying everything from one place meant that the consumer did not need to waste time travelling between different specialist stores, but with the convenience and choice that online shopping gives us, that model doesn't work any more. Woolworths, British Home Stores, House of Fraser and Debenhams all did well in the past.

---

17 JLS Byrnes, *Islands of Profit in a Sea of Red Ink: Why 40% of your business is unprofitable, and how to fix it*

Today, however, many are no longer trading and even before the outbreak of Covid-19 in 2020, others were struggling to survive.

Most small businesses are only likely to make above-average profits if they stay laser-focused on their niche. In an attempt to grow their business, managers can lose that focus. Growing the revenue becomes the objective, on the assumption that all revenue is equally good. This is not the case and it is likely that by trying to serve the wrong clients, or by providing non-core services, profit margins will suffer. Chasing revenue in this way is also likely to be the source of sales and service delivery problems and will be an ineffective use of time.

The television series *Ramsay's Kitchen Nightmares* frequently illustrates this problem in action. The episodes usually start with the celebrity chef Gordon Ramsay going into a failing restaurant, testing a few samples from the menu and swearing a lot. He then has a debrief with the owner, pointing out the various flaws in both the food and their general business acumen which have resulted in the restaurant being in a perilous state.

A common scenario is a restaurant with a menu which is too large and diverse. In one episode, a relatively small restaurant had over 100 items on the menu. To make the kitchen run more smoothly, the owner is often advised to scale down the menu, perhaps to specialise in a certain type of food or to provide a 'chef's special' each day. By reducing the number of items on the menu, the restaurant is more likely to produce better-quality food. Fewer ingredients are needed, which means that they are used more frequently; as a result, the food is fresher and less waste is generated. The staff who prepare the food produce better-quality dishes, as they are more familiar with a smaller number of recipes. It is also possible for the waiting staff to talk about the dishes from experience, having tried all the items on the smaller menu. The clientele who liked a wide variety of dishes on the menu, or whose favourite dishes didn't make the cut, may now go elsewhere. However, the restaurant will begin to make a name for itself in its niche and will attract and retain clients who like the new core products.

Many established small businesses operate more like the restaurant at the beginning of the programme than the version at the end. In their pursuit of any revenue, they expand the menu of services too far to be able to provide a quality delivery. They may also have taken on clients who are too big, too small or for other reasons are not a good fit.

What is your core service?

Your core service may not be the original service that the business was set up to provide, as this might have evolved over time. It may well be where the majority of your revenue comes from, and ideally it will be where you excel or punch above your weight. It should be a service that provides you with an above-average profit margin and a relatively low level of service problems.

As an example, in my consultancy work the core business includes:

- Performance measurement
- Financial strategy
- Planning and analysis
- Raising funds
- Cash management
- Exit planning
- General advice to management

Non-core work would include statutory accounts, tax returns, VAT, bookkeeping, tax planning and independent financial adviser work. I avoid these like the plague.

Who are your ideal clients?

Think about your current clients. Which ones would you love to replicate, and which ones would you ideally not want to do business with? How do the clients you enjoy working with differ from those who you would like to lose? To produce an ideal client profile, you can use the list of characteristics below and any others that are specific to your business:

- Annual revenue
- Number of employees
- Sector
- Age (start-up, growing or established)
- Budget for your services
- Location

My ideal clients fit the following profile:

- Service businesses
- Owner-managed
- Selling to other businesses (B2B not B2C)

- Making annual sales of at least £1 million
- Looking for growth over the next three years
- Solvent (so they can pay my invoices)

With this information clearly in mind, I can generally tell whether a prospective client is likely to be a good fit in a five-minute phone call.

Perhaps surprisingly, a good example of focusing on core business is Amazon. The company is now better known for delivering just about any product to your front door or your drone landing pad. It also provides data services through its Amazon Web Services subsidiary. However, it was set up to provide just one product type through one channel: selling books via the Internet. Amazon did only this for the first five years of its existence, up until 1998. At that point they had grown their revenue from $0 to $1.5 billion. They then 'diversified', adding sales of CDs and DVDs via the same channel.

Volvo is a good example of a large company which chooses to serve an ideal client niche and does not chase revenue from the whole market. The Swedish manufacturer is famous for building cars that are safe. Their research and development, production, marketing and sales are all focused on attracting safety-conscious customers. Rather than chase the whole new-car market and compete with much larger manufacturers, Volvo chooses to focus on this niche. While their sales account for just over 0.5% of sales of all new cars worldwide, Volvo's profit margin of 11.5% made it the third most profitable car maker in the world in 2018.[18] Between 2015 and 2019 they increased sales by 40% from 500,000 to 700,000 adding new production plants in China and the USA.[19]

---

18 S Smith (2018) 'The 20 most profitable car manufacturers', MSN, www.msn.com/en-in/autos/photos/the-20-most-profitable-car-manufacturers/ss-AAq36pf#image=19, accessed 2 August 2020

19 Volvo Media (2016) 'Sales Volumes – Volvo Cars Global Media', www.volvocars.com, www.media.volvocars.com

Client–service matrix

Before moving on to Step Three, use the matrix below to analyse your current client base.

	A	B	C	D
Core				
Non-core				

First, rate each client from A to D on the scale below:

A – Clients who fit your ideal client profile

B – Clients who do not yet fit the profile, but could do in the future

C – Clients who are unlikely to ever fit the profile, but contribute a profitable return

D – Clients who are either unprofitable or too difficult to work with

/global/en-gb/corporate/sales-volumes?year=2015&month=12, accessed 31 August 2020

Start by identifying your larger clients. Which of the eight boxes would you put them in? Look carefully at all the work you are doing which is not in the box on the top left.

An established logistics business followed this exact strategy after a number of years of unfocused revenue growth. They stopped selling services which were incidental to the main business. One particular service had been losing money for years. They also gently moved on a significant number of smaller and hard-to-service clients. Over the following three years, their profits more than doubled.

CASE STUDY PART THREE: DON'T BECOME A BUSY FOOL

Our initial assessment of the tender was that most of the work was similar to our core business. The average order sizes were larger than those of our average customer, but they were similar to those of some of the big clients that we were servicing. This only accounted for 85% of the contract, though.

Deliveries to outlets in Europe and the southern hemisphere would be more challenging for us to service. Added to the geographical challenges, the tender requirements in the UK were also broader than our core business. One example was products with a short shelf-life: in our existing business, we didn't deal with these. It's a specialist sector of the industry, and we decided early on to partner with a specialist supplier.

We changed our operating system to identify these items as each order was taken, and sent a consolidated picking list to our partner for each load. They picked all the orders and delivered them to our warehouse on one pallet for each van on a just-in-time basis.

To service the European outlets, we partnered with a business based in

Frankfurt which specialised in supplying similar clients. As a UK-based operator, this too was clearly non-core business for us, and if we had tried to set up on our own on a tight deadline we would probably have failed.

This was my first experience of the phrase: 'Do what you do best and outsource the rest'. It's a great strategy for any business, but particularly SMEs looking to grow. My company knew how to make a profit in its core business activities and focused on these to build a successful business. In contrast, many SMEs struggle to grow because they assume that they need to do everything themselves and save money, rather than employing experts. The problem is that they get bogged down in the complexities of non-core tasks in which they lack expertise. Focus is lost and the growth suffers. It would be much better to 'stick to the knitting'.

SEVEN

S: Set Growth Objectives

The third step in the CASH process is to set objectives in the form of a medium-term plan. The detailed version of this process generally looks forward three to five years. It produces a forecast to show how the business might look at that time, including a profit and loss account, a responsibilities chart and a company valuation for the end of the period.

In this chapter we will look at the Orbit Planning Tool, which gives some structure to your planning process and ensures that consistent assumptions are made for the key elements of the business.

Setting objectives is a key part of managing any business and a major component of success. However, it is unusual for SMEs to record their objectives in a consistent plan. Communicating such a plan within the business is even more unusual. The only time this does happen regularly is when a business needs to raise cash, because any sophisticated lender will want to see forecasts before parting with their money. However, once the finance has been secured these forecasts are usually filed away, never to see the light of day again – unless, of course, something goes wrong.

Small businesses don't seem to value these formal plans. Among other things they cite a lack of time and resources as reasons to avoid them, but a plan doesn't need to be complicated or take days of management time every year to produce. If the business is aware of its key numbers, it should be straightforward to produce a high-level forecast for twelve months and extend that to three years by making some broad assumptions. The management team should be able to do this in one morning. As an additional benefit, they will align their aspirations and assumptions in the process.

What are your key objectives?

Initially it can be useful to have one key objective which acts as a benchmark for the rest of the planning process.

In my twenties I was interested in sailing and was lucky enough to crew on some private yachts to various destinations in the Mediterranean Sea and beyond. The most adventurous of these was a ten-week trip starting in Cornwall and ending with a classic yacht regatta from the east coast of America back to Bermuda.

On the third day, we had a problem. As we were passing by the Bay of Biscay, the yacht's autopilot malfunctioned and stopped steering the boat. Looking around us, the view was exactly the same in every direction. We must have been a few hundred miles from the nearest land, which was well over the horizon. It was back to basics and we had to take it in turns to manually steer the boat. The only guide we had was a compass. This simple piece of technology, virtually unchanged over hundreds of years, did its job by guiding us in the right direction until the autopilot was fixed some time later.

The one key objective can act like a compass to keep a business on track. Bill Gates' objective to 'Put a PC on every desk in America' is a good example.

Why should you have a plan?

Research from the University of Kent suggests that only one in ten businesses actually produces a formal plan. When asked though, only

50% of those who claim to have a plan can actually find a copy. Therefore, only 5% of the companies surveyed actually use a plan to run their business. Perhaps it's just a coincidence, but a similar proportion – 4% of businesses – grows to exceed an annual turnover of £1 million.[20]

If you run your business without a plan, you don't know where you are going and you won't know when you get there. There are no early warning signs that things are going wrong, or that the business is stagnating and not moving forward as desired. But if there are clear benchmarks to regularly monitor performance against, you are more likely to stay on track. Variances against the plan quickly become clear and something can be done to correct the situation. Good planning will save you time and money.

---

20   S Raby (2015) 'What is good business strategy? The case
     of SMEs', *Kent Business Matters*, https://blogs.kent.ac
     .uk/kent-business-matters/2015/10/02/what-is-good
     -business-strategy-the-case-of-smes, accessed 2 August
     2020

There are some great examples of poor planning on the reality TV programme *Homes Under the Hammer*. The show follows amateur property developers who buy run-down properties at auction before renovating them. The properties are then valued by local estate agents in their pre-renovated condition. The amateur developer transforms the property and (hopefully) sells it for a profit.

A typical example might be a house bought at auction for around £100,000 which has the potential after renovation to be worth £150,000. The amateur developer will then give an estimate of the budget for the renovation, which might be £20,000, resulting in a potential profit of £30,000. Almost invariably this budget includes only the most obvious items, such as kitchens and bathrooms. It will often underestimate the total cost of these and omit a number of other renovation costs that would be obvious had a bit more thought gone into a plan. More often than not, the amateur developers also forget to budget for a contingency.

Once the renovations have been completed and the local estate agents get a chance to update their valuations, the developer talks through their actual spend with the presenter. Occasionally the budget will be about right or even underspent. More likely there will be overruns, many of which could have been predicted with a bit more planning. In most cases a profit is still achieved, but it's smaller than anticipated and no one ever seems to account for the amount of time that the developer has put into the project.

There are some parallels with the way that some small businesses are run. There may well be a basic understanding of costs and revenues, but the expectations for revenues are often over-optimistic and the costs are understated. The result is that the expected profit is squeezed from both ends and sometimes disappears altogether. In some episodes of *Homes Under the Hammer* the developers are only saved by the general increases in the property market which have occurred while their projects dragged on. If a coherent plan had been produced, the profit issues could be understood and managed before they became reality.

Making a plan

Start the planning process by forecasting your future revenues. This is never easy, and owners often say that they can't make a forecast because it depends on the market, the competition, the availability of labour, the cost of raw materials…or they will simply say 'I don't know'.

The object here is not to try and predict exactly what the revenue is going to be for the next few years (unless you do have a crystal ball); it is to make a best estimate backed up by solid assumptions. The only thing that is common in all the forecasts I have done is that they were all wrong. Some were very close, most were close enough, but none were spot on. They were all useful though, as benchmarks to monitor business performance.

If you have specific plans to make a significant change – for example, to add new products or markets – you should add these to the forecast. It is always a good idea to build these assumptions around numbers that you are already measuring. For example, if you currently sell 100,000 units at £10 each, your assumption for the following year might be 120,000 units at £10.50 each. Then if your sales aspirations are not met you can see whether the problem is one of volume, rate or both. If you supply multiple services, you can make individual assumptions for each type.

If a detailed forecast is not possible, you can make a simple assumption for revenue, such as 10% annual growth. The increase should be a stretch, but realistically achievable. Start with the current level of sales (year zero) and forecast forward. If you have significant, unprofitable non-core sales, you might want to plan to reduce those first.

Large businesses are professional and consistent with their objective-setting and planning. Tesla, for example, published its objectives in 2018 for the world to see. The overall goal was to reach a market capitalisation of $650 billion within ten years. At that point, their capitalisation was less than $60 billion. They also published what they called 'operational milestones' showing how the company's revenue would increase from around $10 billion to $175 billion, with profits increasing from $1.5 billion to $14 billion.[21]

Behind the summary information, which was made public, Tesla will have also produced more detailed plans for each year. These would include a budget with assumptions for operating costs, capital expenditure, cash flow, people, factories and sales channels. The assumptions for the first year's sales data will have been broken down by month, model and market, with

---

21 Tesla (2018) 'Tesla announces new long-term performance award for Elon Musk', Tesla.com, https://ir.tesla.com /news-releases/news-release-details/tesla-announces -new-long-term-performance-award-elon-musk, accessed 2 August 2020

different individuals responsible for achieving these numbers.

In 2012 the UK government introduced a £200 million programme called GrowthAccelerator to help England's brightest SMEs achieve their ambition and potential. By the time the scheme closed in 2016, 18,000 businesses had participated in the scheme, and on average they had achieved business growth four times faster than a typical SME. The minimum criterion for joining the scheme was an expectation to double in size over a three-year period.[22] The programme used the Orbit Planning Tool to ensure that the SMEs used a structured method to plot their desired progress over the next three years. An example is shown below.

---

22 K Wright-Whyte (2016) 'Why did the government put the brakes on GrowthAccelerator?', Accounts + Legal, www.accountsandlegal.co.uk/small-business-advice /why-did-the-government-put-the-brakes-on -growthaccelerator, accessed 2 August 2020

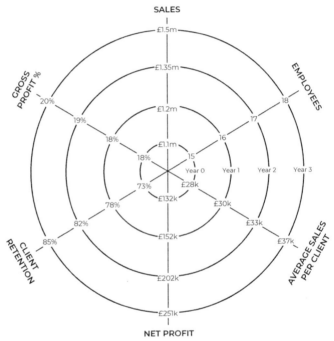

The Orbit Model

Assuming you have completed the exercise earlier in this chapter (forecasting your future revenues), you can fill out the sales axis now. Then consider the other elements of the business that will support this growth, such as activity volumes, employee numbers, new clients, new products or services and new sales channels. Next, consider efficiencies, such as an improved gross profit margin. Finally, consider the level of sales and marketing spend that you will need to achieve your predicted growth.

Some companies only have about half a dozen axes when they do this; others have more than a dozen. What's important is to include all the key elements of the business and make sure that the resulting plan is coherent and consistent.

CASE STUDY PART FOUR: MATCH YOUR AMBITION TO GROW WITH YOUR STRENGTHS AND ABILITIES

To get the project off the ground, we had to present compelling plans to various stakeholders. The customer needed to be convinced that we could deliver the service; our parent company needed to be confident that we could make a profit;

and our partners and sub-contractors needed to understand what was required of them so that they could price their services and gear up their operations.

The tender itself required a detailed plan, which went into a lot of operational detail. This included information about the warehouses, the number of delivery vehicles and the number of personnel. With these key operational numbers, we could produce a financial plan for the business using KPIs from the existing business (eg cost per truck, cost per driver, cost per mile). By adding a profit margin, we were then able to compute the most important number – our price.

Our outsource partners for services, such as a container shipping business, needed data so that we could agree volumes and pricing in advance. We also had to present a five-year plan to our board. They too needed to be convinced that we could deliver the service and provide an acceptable level of profit, while controlling expenditure and without risking the group's reputation.

I was unaware of the Orbit Planning Tool at that time, but it would have been ideal for plotting these business variables and communicating the plan to all of our stakeholders.

EIGHT

H: Hit Your Targets

The fourth and final step is by far the most important. There is no point in having a great plan unless you ensure that it is well executed.

There are two elements to this step. First, ensure that you regularly benchmark and monitor the key numbers in your business over time. This either gives feedback that the business is going in the right direction, or it gives you an early warning that something somewhere is wrong and needs to be rectified – quickly. You can monitor these KPIs in several ways, but the method I have found most effective is to have a visual dashboard of around six key measures. Where possible, these charts should show how each metric is moving over time and compare it to the planned movement and the previous year. The following illustration provides an example.

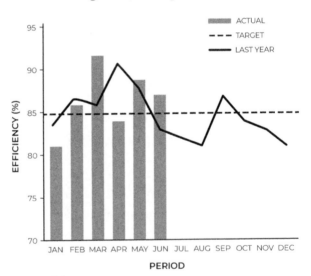

Labour efficiency

A good analogy for this monitoring system is the flight deck used by airline pilots. There are dozens of dials and gauges on the flight deck of a large aircraft, but in the centre are about half a dozen key instruments, which include fuel, altitude, airspeed and a compass. The pilot must ensure that these key instruments are operating within certain tolerance ranges. If any of them go outside these ranges, the pilot knows to look at other, more detailed instruments to identify the cause and resolve the problem.

A well-run business will also identify key measures and monitor them closely to ensure that it stays on the right course.

The second element in this step is to set up a regular meeting with someone who can act as a sounding board. This should be someone who will keep the management team accountable, ask searching questions and generally ensure that the business is moving forward as projected.

For the last twelve years, I've worked with a personal trainer in an attempt to keep fit. The principle is similar. My trainer, Pauline, ensures that I have a regular balanced workout, that I don't skimp on the weights and that I don't finish early. If I have an injury, she ensures that I don't make it any worse. Without that regular appointment I'm sure I would miss more gym sessions, have much less effective workouts and get injured more often.

Research shows that people are more likely to achieve their targets if they make them public and regularly share them with others.[23] 'What gets measured, gets managed' is a popular maxim, which is often true to some extent, but you also need to make sure that you measure the important stuff and take prompt action when something goes wrong.

---

23   B Harkin, et al (2016) 'Does monitoring goal progress promote goal attainment? A meta-analysis of the experimental evidence', *Psychological Bulletin*, 142(2), pp. 198–229

In most large businesses, everything that matters is measured and somebody is responsible for each metric. Small businesses need to do the same thing to ensure that they keep on top of the key elements of the business and take action where necessary. Without regular performance monitoring and feedback from an independent sounding board, your business is far more likely to go off track. Even experienced entrepreneurs can be distracted by the shiny stuff – some new business opportunity which is easier, better or more profitable than the current model. Rather than going off on one of these tangents, SMEs need to focus on finding more ideal clients to buy their core services.

There are various examples of this process on popular television programmes. In *Strictly Come Dancing*, celebrities with little to no dancing experience are fast-tracked over a few short weeks to perform at a high level. Two of the key elements to this process are access to an expert and regular performance monitoring.

The celebrities are given a different dance to perform each week. They are paired up with a professional dancer who has the experience to guide them through the process. At the end of each week they perform a dance and get feedback on various aspects of their performance from a panel of judges. They are scored – sometimes brutally – from one to ten and get some suggestions for improvement in specific areas. The celebrities who improve the most tend to be the ones who go away and work on these suggestions before their next performance.

Compare this to the performance of an average SME. Most do not have systems in place to measure performance in an accurate, relevant and timely manner. Where a reporting system is available, the elements measured are often incomplete and unbalanced. Rarely is there an experienced, independent voice to help guide the entrepreneur.

By the time the contestants get to the final of *Strictly Come Dancing*, the standard of their performances is high and it can be difficult to choose a winner. Imagine what it would be like if one rogue celebrity went through the process on their own, getting a bit of feedback from a friend down at the pub but never being scored by the judges or having a professional to guide them. If they were then to compete in the final, how would they do? Probably not so well. Most of your SME competitors will be operating a bit like this rogue celebrity dancer. If you get this step of the process right, you should easily out-perform the majority of your peers.

How well do you know your KPIs?

Find the KPIs that you need to monitor your business. Different businesses need to measure different metrics, but a balanced set will prob-ably include some of the following:

- Sales volume
- Sales per employee

- Average unit price
- Profit margins
- Labour efficiency
- Labour turnover
- Debtor days
- Cash in the bank
- Client satisfaction

Identify the KPIs in your business. Write down a definition for each one, and assign responsibility to an individual. You can then show them graphically over time on a dashboard.

How do you make yourself accountable?

Accountability is important for achieving the KPIs you have identified. A good example of accountability is the school governor system. While the head teacher and their senior management team are in charge of the day-to-day 'operations' in the school, they are kept accountable by the governing board. There could be ten or twenty unpaid school governors who attend regular board meetings. Detailed minutes are taken by a professional clerk, with action points noted and followed up at future meetings. On joining the board, new governors might be provided with two days' training at the beginning of a four-year term to ensure that they understand their role. This role is clearly communicated and has three key elements:

- To ensure clarity of vision, ethos and strategic direction

- To hold the head teacher to account for the educational performance of the school and its pupils, and for the performance management of staff

- To oversee the financial performance of the school and make sure its money is well spent

Governors are appointed to be 'critical friends'. Their role is to support, guide, challenge and encourage the head teacher. Governors are part of the management team and need to understand the long-term strategic goals of the school. Governing boards might have people with backgrounds in accountancy, banking, child protection, law and property management – all useful skills which could be called on when making decisions about the school's future.

While this level of accountability would not be feasible for most SMEs, there are elements that small businesses could incorporate with the help of a single independent adviser. To ensure your targets are met, schedule at least a couple of hours a month to review progress and look forward. If possible, find someone to act as a sounding board and meet regularly to discuss your progress against the plan and any potential roadblocks to achieving your long-term goals. You might also look for guidance on any high-level strategic issues, but it's important to avoid discussing day-to-day problems.

In a large business, this role might be carried out by a non-executive director: somebody who has a lot of relevant experience and great contacts in the industry. In small businesses, the funds may not be available to employ someone like this. Instead, you could approach an ex-colleague or a family friend who has good business experience and might be prepared to spare some time to act as a sounding board.

CASE STUDY PART FIVE: MEASURE YOUR PERFORMANCE TO HIT TARGETS

This project happened a long time before dashboards came into common use, but we did measure our KPIs. Our performance for each month and the year-to-date numbers were reported and discussed at monthly board meetings. The ratios included average delivery size, the percentage of items that were unavailable at the time of ordering, and average debtor days (how promptly we got paid). Reporting packs were generally in the same standardised form as the rest of our business, which enabled us to compare ourselves to other divisions. This gave us useful information for making improvements. We also had regular customer satisfaction surveys, which gave us good feedback on where we were doing well and where there was room for improvement.

The management team met weekly through the first few months of the business. Once a month the group managing director would join these meetings, acting as our sounding board. Although he had been involved in the project from the start, he only got involved in the major decisions. I can remember thinking that his lack of detailed involvement would be a disadvantage and that we would all know better than him. What I came to appreciate was that his extensive knowledge of the wider sector and his helicopter view of our business meant that he was in an excellent position to hold us accountable. He often saw the big picture when the three of us got lost in the detail.

Not surprisingly, we made a few mistakes along the way. For example, the original estimate for IT expenditure was too low. We needed a new system to manage customs clearances and EU rebates. This was not our core business, and even though we outsourced a lot of the system work our lack of knowledge in this area led to a significant overspend before the contract had even begun. However, we had allowed a significant contingency to cover the unknowns, and thanks to Neil, who was responsible for operations, our final operating procedures were significantly more efficient than the plan we put forward to the client and our board of directors. In our first year the profit was comfortably above the budget.

About a year after setting up this business I decided to move on from the company. My expectations and experience had increased significantly through the process, but by now the new division had settled down and was both stable and profitable. I was lucky to be involved in such a project, and the experience has helped me immensely over the years. Graeme stayed on as Director of Supplies for the remainder of the five-year term and achieved two contract extensions.

NINE

Method Recap

The CASH method is designed to give SMEs some of the tools and processes needed to manage their finances professionally. The method takes best practice from larger organisations and tailors it for use in smaller entities. Implementing the whole method takes time and requires a level of financial expertise that is not usually available in these organisations.

The owner-managers I work with do not need to understand the details of these tools and processes, but they do need to have a high-level understanding of the principles. In this book I have highlighted the key models that help develop a 'profit mindset' and ensure that your business stays focused and profitable while it grows. These are:

1. **Key metrics** to clarify the numbers

2. **A client–service matrix** to focus on the most profitable activities

3. **The Orbit Planning Tool** to produce and communicate a coherent business plan

4. **Dashboards** to formalise a monitoring system for ensuring that the plan is well executed

If the sales and operations elements of your business do not work, these models will not revive a failing business. But if those two elements both work, adding a profit mindset will significantly enhance the overall performance of your business.

TEN

Objections

There are three common excuses for not implementing something as simple and effective as the CASH method.

I haven't got enough time

Barely anyone who runs a business has any spare time. All the successful business owners I have worked with have full diaries, but if they came across an interesting opportunity they would find time to listen.

Spending time now understanding the numbers, focusing on profit, producing a plan and putting a structure in place to ensure that it is executed well will be a great investment. Without this structure in place, it's far more likely that time will be wasted chasing the wrong clients, providing the wrong services and dealing with all the problems that these bad choices produce.

I'm not good with numbers

None of the tools used in this method require any more than a basic understanding of maths. I've not come across anybody who had the ability to build the sales and operations sides of a business but could not understand the basic financial figures and ratios. On the contrary, most entrepreneurs go on to develop a good understanding of profit and loss accounts, balance sheets, cash flow statements and KPIs. You cannot build a profitable organisation without keeping score in the key areas of the business.

I haven't got a crystal ball

Another objection is that people can't produce a forecast because they don't know what the variables are going to be – volume of sales, discounts given or cost per unit, for example. They don't know what's going to happen in the economy over the next year, and it's impossible to know what the competition will be doing.

This is missing the point. There needs to be a target. If you understand your market well enough to risk your time, effort and money on your business, it should be possible to make a reasonable prediction of sales volume, sales prices, cost of sale and expenses.

ELEVEN

Go Do It

It's worth repeating that if you have created a business which has lasted longer than three years and employs a team of staff (however small) then you have already beaten the odds. Don't stop there. Push on and become one of the 4% that achieve £1 million a year in sales. Even better, join the 0.6% who achieve £10 million a year (but only if you are maintaining a good profit margin).[24]

---

24   P Wetherill et al, 'UK business; activity, size and location: 2018'

You now have the tools to create a profit mindset. You owe it to yourself, your family and your team to get a better return for the time and effort that you put into your business. Set aside some time every week to get away from the day-to-day tasks. Find somebody who will act as a sounding board and hold you accountable, and follow the four steps of the CASH method as they apply to your business.

Resources

You now have an overview of the four steps in the CASH method. These are relatively simple concepts, which will help you to structure your commercial decisions in a more rational and profit-driven manner. If you haven't already applied these steps to your business, I urge you to do so now. None of them take long to do, and they are designed to whet your appetite to investigate each area a little further.

Videos

If you'd like extra help with any of these steps, you can find some short videos by visiting www.profitmindsetbook.com. The videos are only a few minutes long and take you through each step using further examples.

Scorecard

A scorecard is also available at www.pareto-fd .com. By answering thirty-two questions about your current business finances, you can use the scorecard to rate your business for each step of the CASH method. It takes less than five minutes to complete and you can measure your progress by taking the scorecard several times at regular intervals.

Acknowledgements

Lots of people have helped me to get this book published. Thank you all:

Graeme Pritchard, for his help on the book.

To all of my beta readers: Richard Morgan, Jo Burfitt, Malcolm Hallsworth, Theo Michaels, Jo Sedley-Burke, Adam Ecclestone and Cathal McCarthy. Thanks for taking the time to read the first draft and give me valuable feedback.

To Lucy McCarraher, Joe Gregory and Kate Latham at Rethink Press, for their advice and encouragement.

Thanks also to all of my clients. It's been a privilege to work with you all.

The Author

Andy Cristin is a finance director with over twenty-five years' experience of working with a broad range of commercial organisations in the UK, Europe and the Middle East.

Andy has worked in two FTSE-listed companies, and another listed on the Euronext Paris. He has also been involved with eleven start-ups, four of which grew from nothing to become multi-million-pound businesses.

In 2008 he founded Pareto Financial Direction Ltd, which focuses on business owners in the B2B services sector, helping them to understand their numbers and build better businesses.

🌐 www.profitmindsetbook.com
www.pareto-fd.com
in www.linkedin.com/in/andycristin